Snack in hand, hat in place, a young lad from Belleplaine pauses on his way home from school to gaze into the camera.

Crane Beach (facing page), the jewel of St. Philip Parish and all Barbados, regularly makes the lists of the world's finest beaches.

A few miles to the west, a catamaran sets sail from the beach at Hastings, in the Parish of Christ Church (above).

The plantation houses which dot the island are perhaps the most striking legacy of the era when "King Sugar" ruled Barbados. Among the oldest is Warrens (above), one of only a handful of "great houses" surviving from the 17th century. The house stands in a grove of mahogany trees near the Warrens roundabout on the ABC Highway and now houses corporate offices.

Barbados

Sun, Sea, Superb!

Text and photographs by

Roger A. LaBrucherie

Imágenes Press

Barbados greets the dawn at Cave Bay, St. Philip, one of a number of superb, secluded beaches along the south coast.

Origins

As my car crests the rise and plunges down Horse Hill road toward the Atlantic shore below, I search the still-dark eastern horizon with a photographer's anxiety: will this dawn bring that just-right balance of clouds and clear sky for a spectacular sunrise? Minutes later, with my tripod set up on the beach, I have my answer, and the sun rises majestically through the mist beyond Bathsheba's coral sentinels, as it has done for eons.

Just when man first witnessed this sometimes stunning scene is impossible to say with precision, but the current evidence suggests that peoples of the Saladoid-Barrancoid culture may have migrated northward to Barbados from their ancestral home in Venezuela's Orinoco Valley as early as the first century B.C. Few traces of their culture have been uncovered in Barbados, but from excavations at other sites they are known to have been primarily an agricultural people, who relied on fishing to supplement their diet.

For the next fourteen centuries the island would be home to Native American peoples—peoples historically referred to as Indians, or, in the anthropologists' word, Amerindians. Those earliest Saladoid-Barrancoid colonizers would, over time, be supplanted by another South American people, the Arawaks, who had established themselves on Barbados by about the eighth century A.D.

The traces the Amerindians left on the landscape were slight, so it is easy to forget the fact that they made Barbados their home for far longer than has the present Euro-African civilization. And yet, when the first English colonists arrived in 1627, there were no people on the island. Why? Because the Indians who had once lived on the island had already fallen victim to another people aggressively exploring and colonizing the Caribbean in the early 16th century: the Europeans.

While Columbus's daring feat of navigation and discovery may have been a heroic advance from the European viewpoint, for the peoples of the New World it was clearly a disaster. The stable world the Indians had known for centuries was suddenly and violently transformed. Within just a few decades of

Although much of Barbados is rolling, level terrain, the island rises gently in a series of terraces toward the east, then falls away steeply to the Atlantic. At the northeastern corner of the island, Cove Bay (known also as Gay's Cove) offers a superb vista of this dramatic coastline.

European "contact," the island populations of the Caribbean had been decimated by warfare, enslavement, loss of lands for hunting, fishing, and farming, and, above all, by exposure to European diseases to which the Indians had no immunity.

On Barbados, the entire Amerindian population had vanished by 1536, when Pedro a Campos, a Portuguese navigator, made the first documented visit to the island, and found it uninhabited. (It is known that there were earlier, unrecorded, Spanish and Portuguese landings, and that the Spanish periodically raided the island in the early 1500s seeking slaves to work their mines and plantations on Cuba and Hispaniola. Some commentators believe that when the Indians realized the threat posed by the Europeans, many fled to their ancestral homeland in South America.)

So after having been home to Indian civilizations for some fifteen hundred years, the island would now lie uninhabited for a century. During that time the island was bypassed by the Spanish and Portuguese, who were too busy with their colonies on the larger islands and the mainland to bother colonizing tiny Barbados. Then, on February 17, 1627, Barbados' century of isolation was brought to an end by the English, when a shipload of settlers aboard the *William and John* landed at Holetown, on the island's west coast. (England's claim to the island had been staked two years earlier, on May 14, 1625, during a chance visit to the island by Captain John Powell.)

The settlers found the island not only uninhabited, but virtually without trace of human habitation, for in the preceding hundred years of isolation the island's lush vegetation had erased nearly every trace of its Amerindian past. Indeed, the only obvious evidence remaining to suggest the Indians' centuries of existence on the island was a crude foot bridge at the site of today's Bridgetown.

Sent out by their sponsor, Sir William Courteen, for the purpose of producing profitable export crops, the English colonists soon cleared land and planted cotton and tobacco. With the help of some Arawak Indians brought from South America, these crops did well, but they soon proved of limited economic value to the colony. Barbados' tobacco proved inferior in quality to that grown in Virginia, while cotton grew well only in the coastal areas of the island.

Fortunately for the colony's proprietors, in 1637 a new crop was introduced from Brazil, where the Dutch and Portuguese had been having great success with it. It was a plant from the grass family, and when properly processed, it would yield a food for which there was great demand in the European diet: sugar. This new crop would have momentous consequences for the island: within a score of years following its introduction, the primeval forest had given way to a sea of sugar cane which nearly covered the island.

Of equal importance were the social, racial, and economic changes sugar would bring. The population of the colony had grown rapidly in its first two decades, and by the 1640s Barbados' population was close to 40,000 people. This population consisted mainly of English yeoman farmers and indentured servants, both drawn by the opportunities offered by cheap land and an open economic system. A small minority of this population (about 15%) were African slaves, employed as domestic help and field laborers on the farms. Had the small-scale farming economy continued, it is easy to speculate that socially, racially, and governmentally, Barbados would have evolved along the lines which eventually developed in the English colonies of North America.

Instead, by the 1660s, just three decades after the introduction of sugar cane to the island, Barbados had developed into a plantation society in which African slaves outnumbered whites two to one. The greatly increased profitability of the land under sugar cultivation attracted heavy capital investment for the purchase of slaves, which, once acquired, were a cheap source of labor. This development placed the small farmer in an impossible competitive situation, and within a few years most had sold out to the larger planters. For the white laboring class the situation was equally bleak. As a result, in the forty years following the introduction of sugar cane, some 30,000 white settlers had left Barbados, emigrating to other Caribbean islands or to North America.

The resulting concentration of economic power in the hands of a very few landowners inevitably meant the concentration of political power as well: by the mid-1700s the island was effectively controlled by a white "plantocracy" of perhaps a hundred families.

Artifacts found at scores of sites around the island (like this baked-clay pot handle, above) bear witness to the Indians who inhabited the island for some fifteen hundred years before the arrival of the Europeans. [The artifact is from the Roach Collection, provided courtesy of Mr & Mrs G. E. V. Clark-Holman, Barbados; shown approximately actual size.]

When the English arrived to settle in 1627, Barbados had lain uninhabited for nearly a century, and was covered with a thick carpet of trees and brush. Within four decades, sugar cane, introduced from Brazil in 1637, had virtually transformed the island: cane fields stretched to the horizon (facing page). Sugar brought with it the plantation system, and so transformed the island's social destiny as well.

Silhouetted against the dawn, the Morgan Lewis Mill in St. Andrew (above) is the island's best-preserved reminder of the era when hundreds of such windmills dotted the landscape, their sails turned to catch the trade winds, grinding around the clock during the harvest season.

Heritage

Thanks to sugar, then, Barbados had become a valuable property to the English Crown, and for a time in the late 1600s was the wealthiest and most profitable of its American colonies. (Until as late as 1700, Barbados' population exceeded that of any of England's North American colonies, with the sole exception of Massachusetts.)

But Barbados' value to the Mother Country was not based solely on her economic importance alone: of equal consideration was the island's militarily strategic location. As the easternmost of the Caribbean islands, Barbados was a natural first port of call for ships coming out from England, and ideally positioned upwind for garrisoning the troops whose duty it was to defend not only Barbados but England's other West Indies possessions as well.

No doubt the presence of those English troops garrisoned on the island helped to keep Barbados free from foreign invasion throughout her history. But as every Barbadian schoolchild knows, of equal importance were the island's natural defenses: coral reefs which nearly ring the island, and Barbados' location on the eastern rim of the Caribbean. In the era of square-rigged sailing ships, when the French, Spanish, Dutch, and English were disputing the region, the prevailing easterly winds made an attack on Barbados from the west a very difficult and time-consuming operation.

Whatever the reason, it cannot be doubted that the unbroken line of peaceful British rule helped instill in Barbadians a pride in British traditions which continues to this day. (Throughout the course of their history Barbadians have never taken offense at being thought "more English than the English," as Barbados' eminent historian, F.A. Hoyos, has put it.)

This long history of things English is reflected in the island's government as well: the country's Parliament dates from 1639, when Governor Henry Hawley set up the House of Assembly. From this beginning, as an essentially consultative body, elected by a tiny minority of propertied whites, the Parliament has evolved over the past three and a half centuries to become the ultimate repository of

As the sugar planters made their fortunes, they built stately homes which became the focal point of their plantations. Like many another historic "great house," Malvern (shown above), one of the loveliest plantation houses in St. John's Parish, now serves as a private residence, independent of the sugar lands which surround it.

The introduction of sugar cane transformed Barbados' destiny by creating a plantation society based on slavery, and for the next two centuries slaves were the backbone of the island's economy. Although the slaves made repeated attempts to throw off their chains, the mass of Barbados' black population remained enslaved until the English Parliament mandated emancipation in 1834. At a roundabout on the ABC Highway, sculptor Karl Broodhagen's statue, entitled "Slave in Revolt", commemorates the slaves' heroic struggle for freedom.

the nation's legislative power, elected by universal adult suffrage. Today an independent nation, Barbados is no longer ruled by a governor, but a largely ceremonial governor-general continues to represent the British monarch. For when Barbadians chose independence in 1966, they also elected to remain within the British Commonwealth, and Queen Elizabeth II is Barbados' head of state as well as England's.

The executive functions are exercised by the Cabinet, headed by the Prime Minister (the Governor-General is required to appoint as Prime Minister the person best able to command a majority in the House of Assembly), who then advises the Governor-General on the selection of the remainder of the Cabinet.

A heritage of slavery

Early in my researches into Barbadian history, I had visited the archives of St. Michael's Cathedral in Bridgetown, and there had come upon a fascinating record of another aspect of the island's past, revealed in ancient parish burial registers. There, on pages from the early 1800s, were the entries that recalled the era when the great mass of Barbados' inhabitants were the slaves who worked its plantations and performed its domestic chores. The books preserved, in a careful hand, the entries the registrar had made nearly

two centuries before: the names of each deceased, and, in the case of blacks and mulattos, their color and civil condition: "Charlotte Lloyd (free negro)," "Sarah (slave)," "Joseph Harris [white]," "Nancy (slave)," "Elizabeth Hughes (free mul.)," "Dinah (slave)" . . ..

Indeed, Barbados' history of slavery dates from the birth of the colony itself, for among the founding colonists aboard the *William and John* when it dropped anchor off Holetown in 1627 were ten African slaves taken from a Portuguese ship captured on the voyage out from England.

As we have seen, the subsequent introduction of sugar cane cultivation led to a "plantocracy" consisting of an enormous slave population ruled by a tiny white planter minority. Although this plantocracy originated in an economic system, its influence was of course not limited to the economy. And since the plantocracy was of English stock, it goes without saying that English values dominated Barbados' social and cultural landscape. It was a domination which persisted not only during the slave era, but for long after emancipation brought slavery to an end.

So while the seeds of Barbados' African cultural heritage date back to the earliest days of the colony, they had never been able to flourish. It is hardly surprising, then, that as the island's society has become truly democratic during the past few decades, many Barbadians have come to question the country's traditional identification with her British heritage—an identification so profound as to have virtually denied the African cultural roots of the vast majority of her people.

Few have carried such questioning as far as the tiny minority of young Barbadians who have adopted Rastafarianism as religion and lifestyle. Tracing its origin to Jamaica, Rastafarianism rejects much of European-based culture and religion as materialistic and untrue to Biblical dictates. Rastafarian doctrine asserts the divinity of Ethiopia's Haile Selassie and espouses the return of the black race to Africa. Such beliefs, coupled with the Rastas' unorthodox appearance and lifestyle—including the famous dreadlocks resulting from unshorn hair, communal living arrangements, and the use of "ganja" (marijuana)—have made Rastafarians a controversial element in Barbadian society.

To most Barbadians, Rastafarianism remains an extreme rejectionist position. Still, a good many Barbadians have come to feel that, in emphasizing its British tradition, the nation long neglected the African and Caribbean influences which are very much a part of its history. In the past few years there has been broad community support for groups such as Yoruba House and DePAM (De People's Art Movement), as well as for individual artists of all disciplines, who have attempted to bring to life—in drama, dance, music, and art—Barbados' African traditions. This flowering of her African side has perhaps been a long time in coming; but in this enthusiastic embrace of its entire heritage, modern Barbados reveals the self-confidence and maturity which have long distinguished her people.

A Barbadian landmark, Codrington College overlooks Conset Bay in St. John. The college is a theological institution for the education of West Indian clergy, and was created from the bequest of plantation owner Christopher Codrington, following his death in 1710.

No Caribbean isle would be complete without its pirate story: according to the legend, in the early 1800s Samuel Hall Lord took to "wrecking" ships on the island's reefs by hanging lanterns in coconut trees along the shore. Then Sam and his cohorts would overpower the crew and loot the ship.

Historians call the legend baseless, but somehow around 1820 Sam Lord acquired the funds to build a large white house overlooking Long Bay in St. Philip. Legend and architectural style soon combined to make the house a "castle," and a castle it has remained (facing page). And on warm Caribbean evenings the romance of Sam Lord's Castle and its splendid setting conspire to lend credence to old Sam's legend as well. (Today Sam Lord's Castle serves as the centerpiece for a large resort hotel.)

In a bygone day, Barbados was a key outpost for defending Britain's Caribbean colonies, and in 1868 a British officer carved "the Lion" on the hillside below the Gun Hill Signal Station. Though the Empire is gone, the coral statue remains, a reminder of the era when Britain's might stretched around the globe.

King Sugar

Sugar. For over three centuries, sugar *was* Barbados: the landscape was one of unending cane fields, and sugar growing and processing were at the heart of all Barbadian economic, social, and political life. Indeed, so well suited are Barbados' soil, wind, sunshine, rainfall, and topography to the growing of cane that to this day no crop better adapted to the island's conditions has been found to supplant it.

And yet today, the Barbadian sugar industry is on its last legs, beset by falling world sugar prices and increasingly unable to compete with other sugar-producing areas of the world where land prices, wage rates, and other operating costs are far below those on the island.

As recently as the 1930s, over one hundred sugar factories dotted the landscape; as of this writing, only three continue operating. And while it is true that much of this consolidation came about for sound economic reasons, the fact is that by every measure Barbados' sugar industry is but a shadow of its former self. The country has already "lost" many thousands of acres of its cane land, much of it to industrial and residential development, while even more has been converted to pasture, or simply lies fallow, for want of a suitable crop which can be profitably grown.

Given the loss of cane land in recent years, a return to the record production levels of the 1950s and 1960s, when sugar production twice exceeded 200,000 tons, is a virtual impossibility. After years of decline and losses, it hard to recall the age when sugar was "king" on the island, and many have taken to wondering for how much longer the island's cane fields and sugar factories—for centuries the very essence of Barbados' landscape and economy—will survive.

Fortunately for the nation's work force, the decline of the sugar industry has been offset by robust growth in other areas of the economy. For example, by 1970, manufacturing had overtaken agriculture as a percentage of the gross national product. (This very rapid economic transformation can hardly be

The spread of sugar cane cultivation created a landscape reminiscent of the Mother Country, and in time, people took to calling the island "Little England." (The photograph here, taken in 1980, overlooks the parish of St. Philip.)

overstated: as recently as 1946, agriculture accounted for nearly half of the island's gross domestic product; by 1991, it was less than 6%.) This shift away from agriculture has hardly been an accident, for Barbadians have an historic aversion to agricultural labor, dating back to the era of slavery.

In the face of this long-term economic transition, an increasingly activist government policy has sought since the 1950s to reduce the high unemployment rates and economic instability inherent in a sugar monoculture. One part of that governmental policy has promoted the establishment of scores of local "enclave" manufacturing operations by foreign companies. Employing Barbadian manpower, the firms import raw materials duty free, then export the assembled product, and pay no income taxes on their profits during a "tax holiday" period. While the program has not been without its problems, there is no doubting its overall success, and it has contributed significantly to reducing unemployment and diversifying the economy.

For three hundred years Barbados' economy *was* sugar. But the Barbadian economy of today is increasingly diversified, and in addition to the now well-established manufacturing sector, technical and business services such as banking, insurance, accounting, and information processing are growing in importance. And with the ever-growing sophistication of the Barbadian labor force, these sectors are now overtaking tourism, the industry whose explosive growth during the 1960s "rescued" the island from King Sugar's decline.

The increasing scarcity of laborers to do the hard work of the sugar cane harvest has led to the introduction of ever more machinery in the fields (above).

Apart from the cane fields themselves, nothing so embodies the sugar industry as the island's sugar "factories", and their heavy sweet molasses smell is familiar to anyone who has visited Barbados during harvest season. (The photograph on the facing page, taken in the mid-1980s, shows the Bulkeley Factory in St. George Parish; by the early 1990s its future was in doubt.)

Today a mere handful of factories continue operating, and the abandoned, shuttered factories found across the island stand as forlorn symbols of a great industry's decline.

During the height of King Sugar's reign, the completion of the harvest season brought singing, dancing, and general merriment to mark the end of the crop. While those plantation celebrations are now a thing of the past, the traditional festivities have been given a new birth in an annual summer-time "Crop Over" celebration involving island residents and tourists alike.

The modern version adds street fairs, dramatic performances, and calypso competitions, and culminates in Kadooment (these pages)—a Carnival-like "jump" through the streets of Bridgetown featuring steel bands, gaudy costumes, and plenty of rum to smooth the way.

VEXX

With King Sugar's decline, thousands of acres of sugar cane and thousands of sugar industry jobs vanished. Some of that former cane land is now used for growing vegetables, like this St. Philip field where Wilma Straughn (above) bags beets for the local market.

Like Mrs. Straughn, drill-rig roustabout Junior "Rambo" Hamilton (facing page) also works in a former cane field: since the 1980s the development of oil and gas wells have made drilling rigs a common sight in the cane fields around Woodbourne, Christ Church.

Island in the Sun

While sugar is at the core of Barbados' history, and the country has made considerable strides toward industrial diversification, the fact remains that it is the island's "sun, sand, and sea" that have gained her renown throughout the world. Of course, the island has always enjoyed these blessings in abundance, but not until the middle of this century did they become a veritable gold mine for the country.

Perhaps the most important cause of this development was a shift in attitudes in Europe and North America toward lying in the sun and acquiring a tan—once regarded as the exclusive activities of "mad dogs and Englishmen." That change, together with the enormous growth in disposable income among people in the USA, Canada, and Western Europe, along with the advent of mass air travel, made the idea of journeying thousands of miles for a vacation a feasible prospect for large numbers of people.

Tourism has helped raise Barbadians to an unprecedented level of prosperity—a prosperity all the more valued because for the first time in the island's history it is spread among all levels of society. But tourism has brought problems as well. The rapid growth of tourism in the 1960s and 1970s frequently led to overcrowding in public services, such as the airport and bus system, and resulted in uncontrolled building in the coastal areas. Also, perhaps inevitably in a country where annual tourist arrivals have in some years outnumbered the population two to one, Barbados' tradition of courtesy, based on the closeness of a small community, has come

A warm winter afternoon brings tourists and locals alike flocking to the south coast's Accra Beach, a spot especially popular with the younger set.

Fringed with coconut palms, a superb west coast beach near Gibbs Bay, St. Peter, epitomizes the island's tropical splendor. In 1956 Barbados provided the setting for the filming of the movie **Island in the Sun**, *based on the famous novel by Alec Waugh.*

under severe strain. Tourists bring jobs and dollars, but they also bring new ideas and new mores, which may be at great variance with those of a traditional society. All in all, Bajans have managed the onslaught well; there is a great gentleness in the people, and the famous respectfulness of the Bajan nature extends to a respect for different ways as well. And the fact that that respectfulness is founded on a fundamental *self*-respect has provided a steadying influence in a sea of outside influences.

Hopefully the tourist, coming from societies where material wealth often engenders notions of cultural superiority as well, also learns from the contact. The tourist may learn something of the value of a slower pace of life, and be reminded of the warmth and security of close-knit communities often only a memory in the larger world outside. Indeed, the contact may lead him to a healthy questioning of the direction of his own society—and that, perhaps, may ultimately mean much more than a carefully acquired suntan.

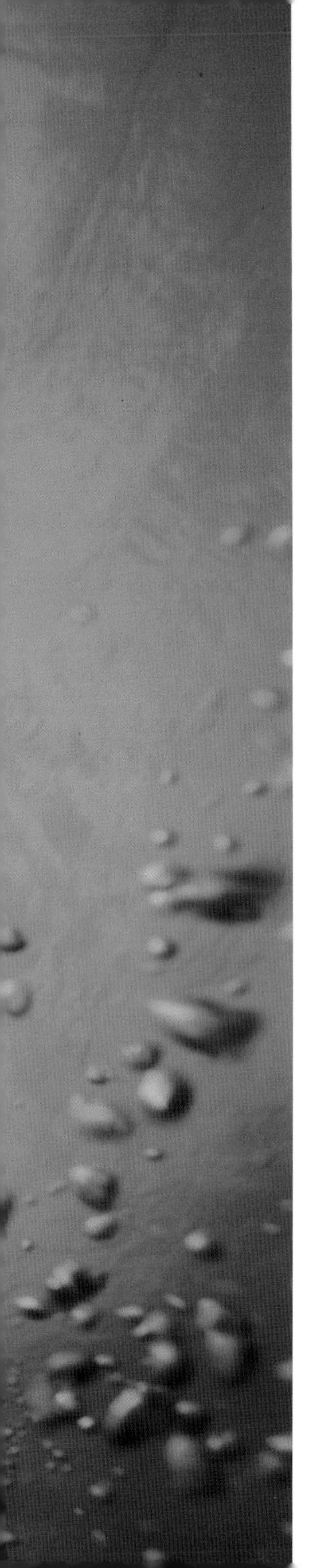

When a sun-lover tires of lying on the beach, there's always the water; and in addition to the sports available on the surface, for those willing to dive below, there awaits a visual treasure among the reefs off the island's southern and western coasts. Here (facing page) a Scuba diver rises to the surface from a dive on a wreck near Holetown.

The island's waters are as alluring to her residents as they are to visitors: a young fisherman from St. James Parish tests the sun-sparkled waters of Payne's Bay with a handline (above).

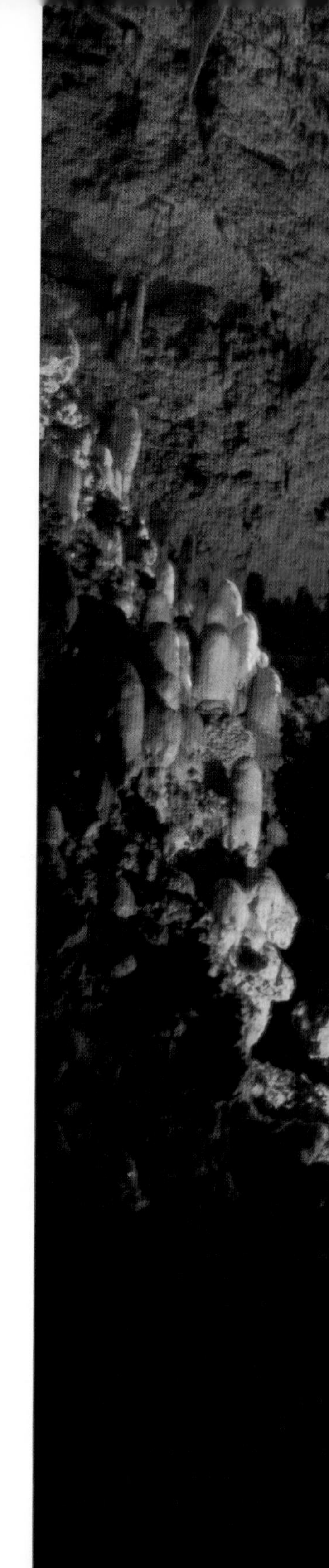

Whether exploring the island or heading to the local minimart, tourists like to get there in the open air. (The Australian-made MiniMoke shown above, long the mainstay of tourist rental vehicles, is now giving way to more modern replacements.)

Moving at a slower pace, visitors riding in electric trams explore Harrison's Cave, reputedly the largest limestone cavern in the West Indies (facing page). Since its opening in the early 1980s, the spectacular cave has become the island's most popular tourist attraction. The trams are part of a climate-control system designed to protect the caverns against the pollution which could damage the delicate formations.

The beautiful, broad beaches and quiet waters of the west coast make it ideal for lazing on the beach, and it is here where most of the island's luxury hotels and splendid private vacation homes are found.

But while Barbados is world famous for her beaches, it is the warmth and hospitality of her people that make the island a special place, and indeed, it is the friendliness of the Barbadian people which is most often cited by visitors when they are asked what they most like about the island. [Photograph above by W. Woodworth/SuperStock]

16
9115

A cruise ship docked in Bridgetown's Deepwater Harbour gleams under the winter sun (facing page). The past few years have brought a phenomenal growth in cruise ship visitors. Whether cruise ship passengers or stay-over visitors, the tremendous influx of tourists make it easy to sympathize with a resident's whimsical identity statement (above).

ONARCH OF THE SEAS
OSLO

Bajan

A young Bajan schoolgirl enjoys a lollypop on Games Day at her primary school in Belleplaine, St. Andrew. (The term "Bajan" is the oft-heard short form, both adjective and noun, for "Barbadian.")

No Barbadian buildings so gracefully combine beauty and historical significance as do her parish churches, and St. John's (above), has always been my personal favorite. Perched at the edge of Hackleton's Cliff, the view from its churchyard of the Atlantic coast below is breathtaking. (The present church building, the fifth on the site, dates from 1836.)

I first came to know Mrs. Iris Humphrey on my first visit to Barbados, when I was staying just down the road in Top Rock, Christ Church. Her cheery "Hello, darlin' " each time I passed by her little chattel house came to epitomize Bajan friendliness for me.

Older Barbadians are often reluctant to be photographed, but youngsters are usually a different story: these schoolboys from Martin's Bay, St. John's Parish, happily posed for me one morning while walking to school.

An aerial view of the west coast near Holetown (facing page). The west coast was historically shunned by Barbadians, because it seldom feels the trade winds which cool much of the island. Today, air conditioning and mosquito control have combined to help make this area the Barbadian "Gold Coast"—the most coveted real estate on the island.

Only a few years ago, this hillside pasture in St. Andrew (above) would have been covered with sugar cane. With the decline of the sugar industry, many areas like this one have been converted into grasslands for pasturing cattle.

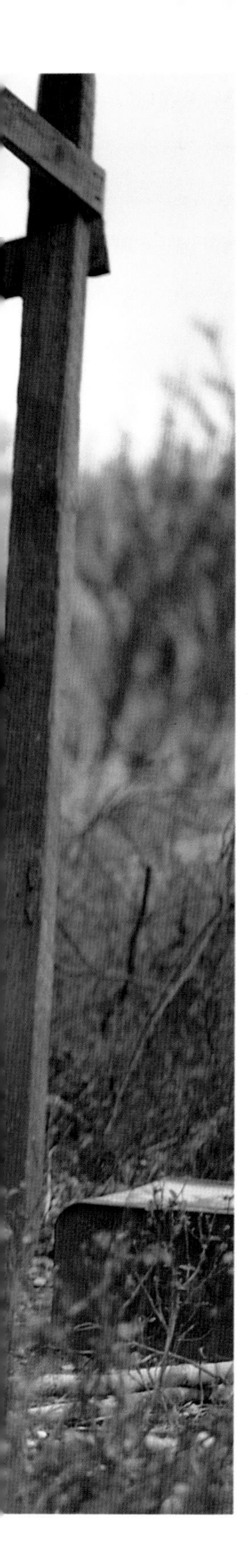

As I drove past these children standing by the road near Six Cross Roads, St. Philip (facing page), I couldn't resist their shouted request to "Take my picture!"

A road repair crewman (above) pauses on his way to work in St. Andrew's Parish. An extensive public works program has provided the country an excellent road system, as well as reducing the unemployment resulting from the sugar industry's decline.

One of the jewels of Barbadian plantation houses, Villa Nova (facing page), nestles in six acres of garden and woods in St. John Parish. The house dates from 1834, taking its name (meaning "New House") from the fact that it replaced the earlier plantation house destroyed in the great hurricane of 1831.

While plantation houses were usually built inland, surrounded by their sugar lands, more recent builders of fine Barbadian homes have often sought out seaside locations. One of the most charming of these, in both setting and architecture, is Mango Bay (above). Located on the shore in St. James, Mango Bay is one of several buildings on the island designed, remodeled, or decorated by the late Oliver Messel (famed for his set design for London stage productions, including "My Fair Lady").

The west coast's pristine beaches and gentle waters have made it a tourist haven (above). But long before overseas visitors made the island their winter playground, Bajans themselves favored the bracing breezes of the area around Bathsheba, on the east coast (facing page). To this day, many islanders prefer this wild and often lonely eastern shore, with its breakers rolling in unimpeded from the Atlantic, as their place to "get away."

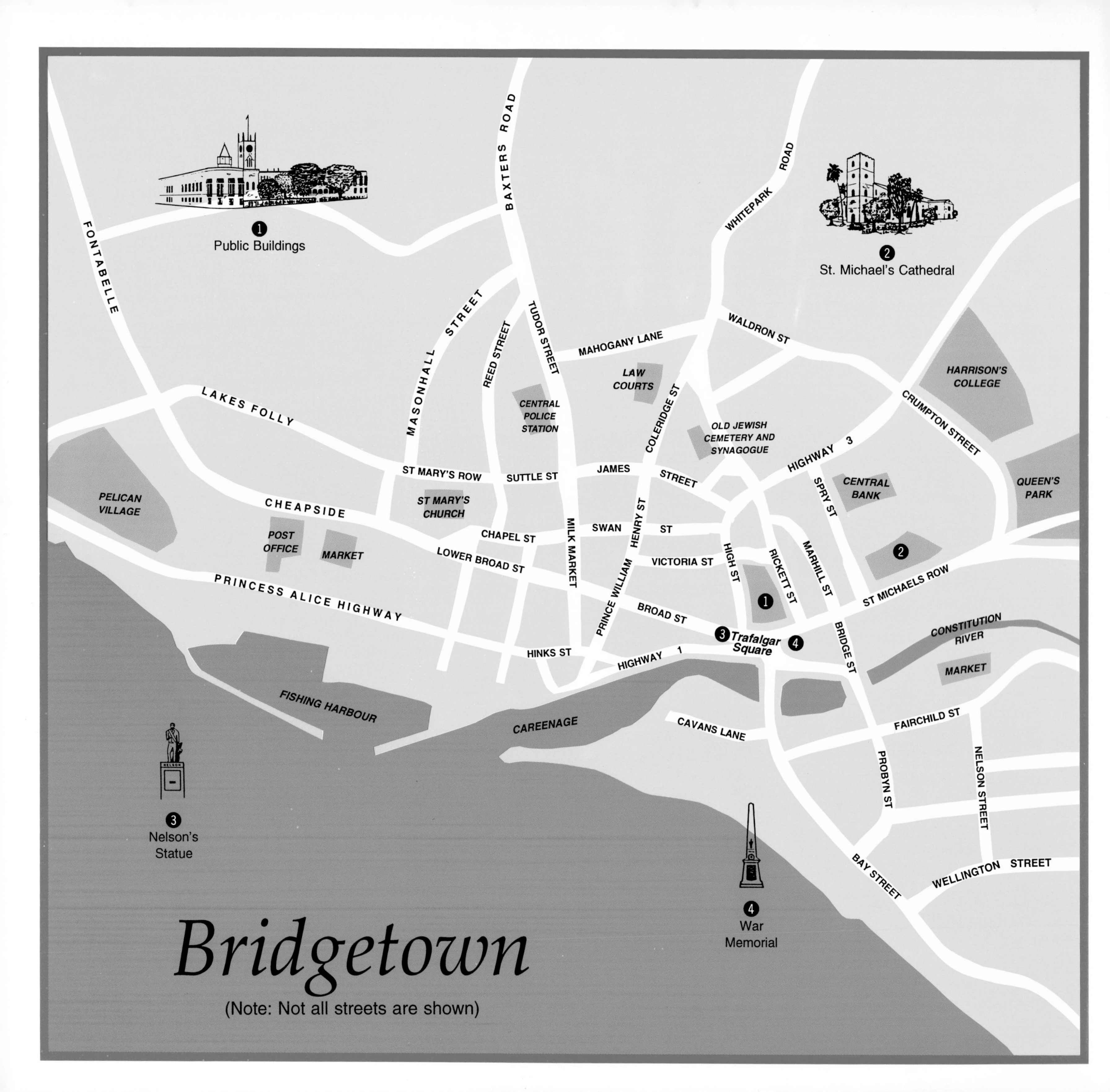

Bridgetown

(Note: Not all streets are shown)

Bridgetown

Centered around its famous Careenage and adjacent Trafalgar Square, Bridgetown dates from the earliest years of the island's settlement as an English colony, for there are records of houses on the site from 1628 onward. Although the settlement at Holetown preceded it by a year, it was the superiority of the Careenage and Carlisle Bay as a port which soon made Bridgetown the island's principal town and capital.

The bridge which inspired the city's name antedates the colonization of the island, for when the English arrived to settle in 1627, they found the remains of a crude foot bridge left by the Indians who had long inhabited Barbados. Indeed, "The Indian Bridge Towne" was one of the town's earliest names. Among other early names, before the present one was settled on, were "The Bridge," "The Bridge Town," and "St. Michael's Town."

Just when the city's central plaza took on the somewhat grandiose name "Trafalgar Square" is uncertain, but it probably dates from soon after 1813, when Barbadians erected the statue of Lord Nelson which graces the square to this day. A number of the street names in the central area (Swan, High, James, and Tudor, to name a few) also date from the city's earliest years, although the combination of fire, hurricane and wooden construction resulted in the destruction of the earliest buildings long ago. Although much of "old" Bridgetown dates from the mid-19th century, one very old building which has survived is St. Michael's Cathedral, built in 1789. The neo-Gothic Parliament Buildings, despite their appearance of great antiquity, were not erected until the 1870s, following the great fire of 1860.

In the past few decades, the decline in farming as a way of life, plus the growth of industry and government, together with the convenience of urban living, have swelled the population of the city. Today the Bridgetown metropolitan area, which extends far beyond the rather modest city limits, contains well over 100,000 people—about 40% of the island's total population.

Bridgetown spreads out from the Careenage (facing page), the narrow waterway which gave birth to the city. The Careenage takes its name from the fact that on its once-sloping banks wooden-hulled sailing vessels were in bygone years "careened" (rolled onto their sides) for repairs.

At the heart of the city is Trafalgar Square (above). The Square witnesses a colorful and varied daily parade: office and shop workers on their way to work in the Broad Street area; tourists exploring the Careenage and Parliament Buildings; vegetable vendors passing through to their usual sidewalk stations, their heads bearing their wares; schoolchildren cavorting on their way to and from the bus stands; and taxi drivers on the lookout for passengers.

ROYAL
OF CANADA

The Chamberlain Bridge, or "Swing Bridge," spans the Careenage and provides the direct route into the city center from the south (facing page).

Just across the bridge, Lord Nelson has stood guard over Trafalgar Square since 1813 (above). The square is named to commemorate the admiral's famous sea battle, where England's greatest naval hero gained victory, but lost his life, in 1805.

DA COSTA & Co
HARRISONS
BNB
COLONNADE
MALL
SUZUKI

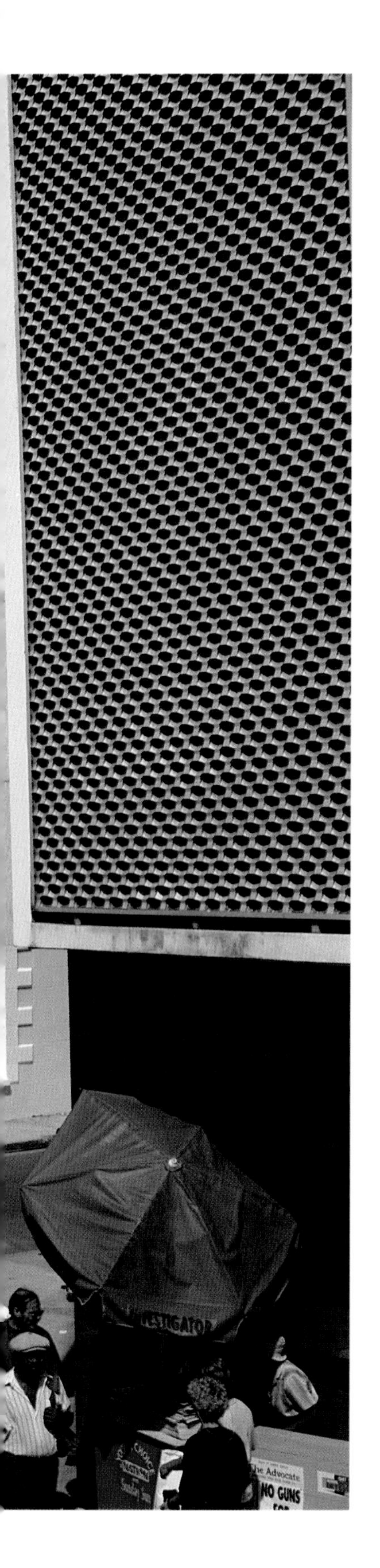

Broad Street, the city's most prestigious shopping, banking, and business district, is lined with a potpourri of architectural styles (facing page). Perhaps the street's most beautiful structures are the colonnaded Da Costa Building (the two-storey building in the foreground), and just beyond, its taller contemporary, the Harrison's Building.

Another architectural gem, Queen's Park House (above), is set in Queen's Park, a green oasis on the eastern edge of the city center. Built circa 1786 as the residence for the island's commanding general, today Queen's Park House houses an art gallery and theatre.

Much of the city's character is provided by her aged, balconied, wooden buildings, like those on Baxter's Road (the photograph on the facing page was taken in the early 1980s). Although more picturesque old buildings are demolished each year to make way for modern structures, enough remain to provide a bit of shade for the city's venerable fruit and vegetable hawkers (above). Despite repeated attempts to relocate them into central markets, these sidewalk merchants have a long history on their side, and seem determined and likely to remain a colorful part of the city scene for many years to come.

CYNTHIA'S
Beauty Salon
PHONE
HOUSE
OF
BARGAINS
PHONE
65919

Barbadiana

As the "English pub of the tropics", the Barbadian rum shop is invariably the informal social center of the neighborhood. The steps of this one near Speightstown provide the ideal spot for "limin' out" on a Friday afternoon.

In the push to modernization, much the island's charming architecture is disappearing. This colorful building on Bridgetown's Suttle Street appeared in my first book on the island, Images of Barbados, *published in 1979. To my regret, it was torn down sometime in the late 1980s.*

Pursuing a time-honored Bajan pastime, a woman surveys the passing scene from the window of her roadside chattel house near Mount Gay, St. Lucy.

The camera brings forth a smile from this young lady in her classroom at the Clifton Hill primary school in St. Thomas. A system of free, universal education produces a populace with a near-100% literacy rate.

After her beaches, perhaps no aspect of the Bajan landscape so charms the visitor as her omnipresent chattel houses (above). The term "chattel house" stems from the fact that, historically, rural Bajans owned their houses, but not the land on which they rest. Hence the term "chattel," an archaic word denoting movable property, as opposed to real estate.

Although undoubtedly there are no two exactly alike, chattel houses are generally of single-wall, lap-board wood siding construction, with a corrugated metal roof (typically peaked and painted red). The houses

often sit on very rustic foundations—sometimes nothing more than carefully chosen rocks piled one on another!

Despite their charm, the Barbadian chattel house is slowly disappearing: as Bajans move "up" in the world, they usually want a "wall" house constructed of concrete block. Perhaps it is fortunate, then, that the chattel house style is enjoying a modern rebirth, seen more and more in small commercial buildings, like this tourist shopping "village" in St. Lawrence Gap, Christ Church (above).

As recently as the early 1980s, small inter-island steamers commonly known as "banana boats" would from time to time dock in the Careenage, and the wharf would become an instant open-air market as fruit vendors descended to the dock to haggle for the best prices.

Still widely in use only three decades ago, the donkey cart has now all but disappeared. (I photographed the one above in 1984.) A few carts remain, continuing to haul an occasional cargo like this load of cane "meat" (the tops and leaves of the sugar cane which are cut off and left in the field at harvest time), which is used as fodder for livestock.

In Barbados, cricket season lasts from January to December: here a match plays out on a summer afternoon on the field before the St. George's Parish Church (facing page).

One of the world's greatest cricket "all-rounders" ever, Sir Garfield "Gary" Sobers poses in the Mecca of Barbadian cricket, the Kensington Oval (above). During the 1950s and '60s he rose to greatness, joining the Barbadian cricketing pantheon inhabited by George Challenor, Herman Griffith, and the "Terrible Three W's": Clyde Walcott, Everton Weekes, and Sir Frank Worrell. In 1975 he became Sir Garfield, when Queen Elizabeth II knighted him before a cheering crowd at the Garrison Savannah.

Pictured above is the national flower: "Pride of Barbados" (Caesalpinia pulcherrima), also known as the dwarf poinciana.

On a hillside in St. Joseph overlooking Bathsheba and the Atlantic Ocean, Andromeda Tropical Gardens (facing page) unites a superb collection of plants in a natural setting. Established in 1954 by the late Mrs. Iris Bannochie, the gardens are now one of the several properties owned and operated by the Barbados National Trust, an organization dedicated to the preservation of the island's natural and historic heritage.

Selected Places of Interest

NOTE: The numbers refer to the numbers on the map; check locally for schedules and entrance fees.

1. BRIDGETOWN AND ENVIRONS: A glance at a map will show that (nearly) all roads lead to Bridgetown, and with good reason: the capital is the commercial, cultural, and governmental heart of the island. At or near the city center are TRAFALGAR SQUARE, the CAREENAGE, the PARLIAMENT BUILDINGS, ST. MARY'S CHURCH, the OLD SYNAGOGUE, ST. MICHAEL'S CATHEDRAL, and QUEEN'S PARK. BROAD STREET is the principal shopping district. To the south, along Bay Street and Highway 7, lies the GARRISON SAVANNAH, surrounded by a number of buildings of architectural and historic interest, including the excellent BARBADOS MUSEUM.

2. OISTINS: The village of Oistins is one of the island's historic towns, dating from the first half of the 17th century. In the early days of the island, before a modern highway system centralized ocean shipping from Bridgetown, Oistins was a significant port. Today the vessels are fishing boats, and during Easter Oistins hosts its annual FISH FESTIVAL.

3. THE CRANE: Another of the bygone ports, where a crane once stood to load ships serving the parish of St. Philip. Today the name identifies the island's most famous beach and the hotel that overlooks it.

4. SAM LORD'S CASTLE: Once the home of the legendary Samuel Hall Lord (see the "Heritage" chapter), today the centerpiece of a luxury hotel.

5. CODRINGTON COLLEGE: The east coast's most famous landmark, Codrington stands at the end of an avenue of cabbage palms, and dates from the early 18th century.

6. ST. JOHN'S CHURCH: The island is divided into eleven parishes, each with its own (Anglican) parish church. St. John's stands in quiet splendor high on the edge of HACKLETON'S CLIFF. The churchyard offers a truly glorious view of the east coast.

7. THE FLOWER FOREST & ANDROMEDA GARDENS: Two superb gardens with a vast display of the flowers, shrubs, and trees of the tropics.

8. BATHSHEBA AND THE EAST COAST: Traditionally the Bajans' favored vacation area, the crashing waves of this windswept shore evoke the slower pace of a bygone era.

9. THE SCOTLAND DISTRICT: The dramatically eroded hillsides of the parish of St. Andrew offer a startling contrast to the rolling hills of most of the island. The MORGAN LEWIS WINDMILL is the sole sugar windmill to survive with its arms and grinding machinery intact.

10. PLANTATION HOUSES: Foremost among Barbados' architectural treasures are her plantation "great houses," a few of which date from the mid-1600s. ST. NICHOLAS ABBEY, VILLA NOVA, SUNBURY, and FRANCIA are open for public tours.

11. BARBADOS WILDLIFE RESERVE: A grove of mahogany trees shelters this wildlife sanctuary, where visitors can catch more than a fleeting glimpse of the green monkeys which roam wild throughout the island's woodlands.

12. SPEIGHTSTOWN: For many decades of the island's early history this was a thriving port and whaling center. The town retains a number of historic and picturesque buildings reminiscent of the era when it was known as "Little Bristol."

13. HOLETOWN: It was here, when the *William and John* dropped anchor in February, 1627, that Barbados' history as an English colony began, and Holetown is the island's oldest settlement, predating Bridgetown by a year. The town is the center of activity on the west coast, and each February the annual HOLETOWN FESTIVAL commemorates the town's role in Barbadian history

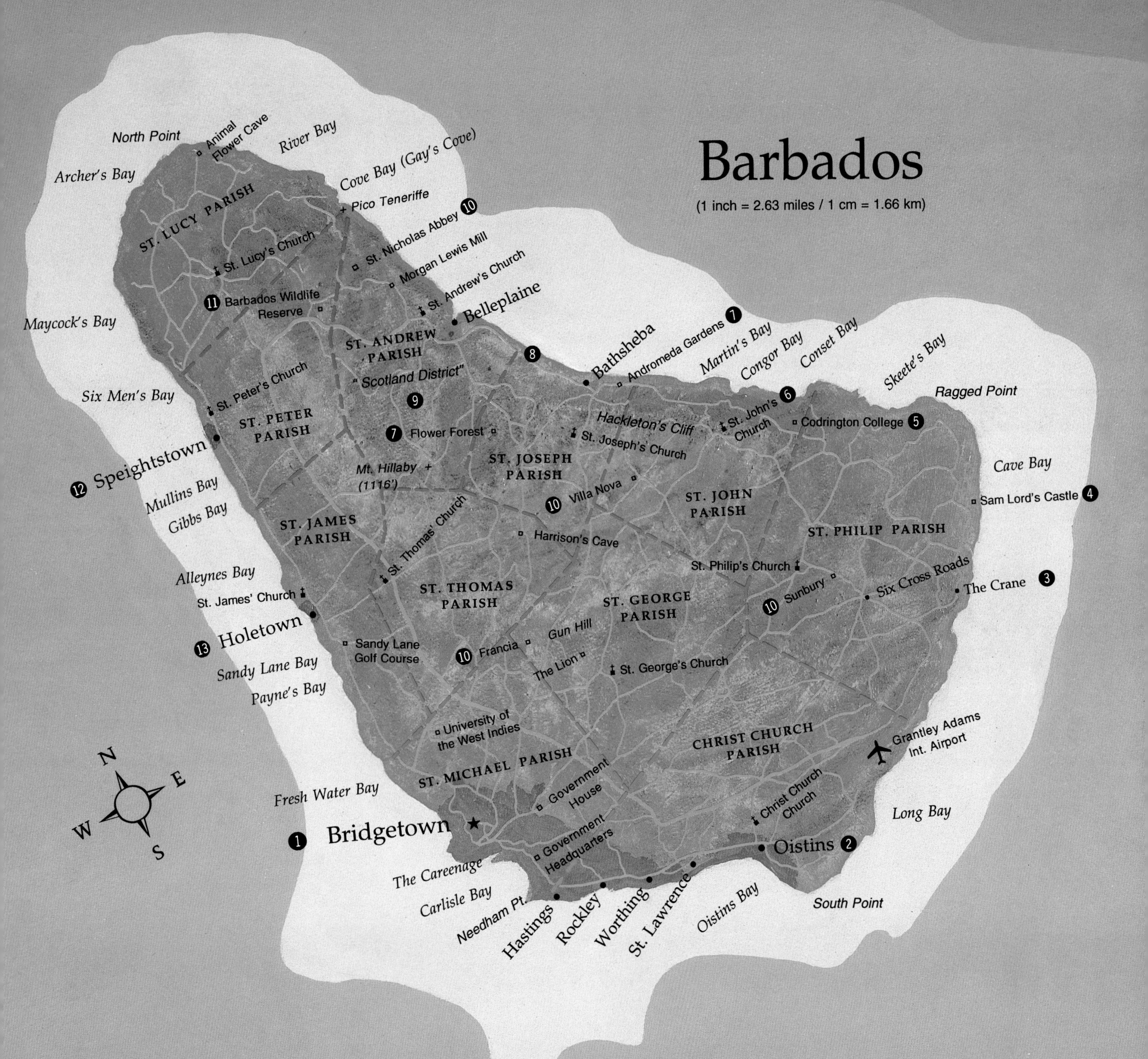

Barbados
(1 inch = 2.63 miles / 1 cm = 1.66 km)
North Point
Animal Flower Cave
River Bay
Archer's Bay
Cove Bay (Gay's Cove)
Pico Teneriffe
ST. LUCY PARISH
St. Nicholas Abbey 10
St. Lucy's Church
Morgan Lewis Mill
St. Andrew's Church
11 Barbados Wildlife Reserve
Belleplaine
Maycock's Bay
ST. ANDREW PARISH
1 Andromeda Gardens
Bathsheba
Martin's Bay
Congor Bay
Conset Bay
8
"Scotland District"
Skeete's Bay
Six Men's Bay
St. Peter's Church
9
Ragged Point
6
ST. PETER PARISH
Hackleton's Cliff
St. John's Church
Codrington College 5
7 Flower Forest
St. Joseph's Church
12 Speightstown
ST. JOSEPH PARISH
Mt. Hillaby (1116')
Cave Bay
Mullins Bay
10 Villa Nova
Sam Lord's Castle 4
Gibbs Bay
ST. JOHN PARISH
ST. JAMES PARISH
St. Thomas' Church
Harrison's Cave
ST. PHILIP PARISH
Alleynes Bay
St. Philip's Church
Six Cross Roads
3
St. James' Church
ST. THOMAS PARISH
10 Sunbury
The Crane
ST. GEORGE PARISH
13 Holetown
Sandy Lane Golf Course
Gun Hill
10 Francia
The Lion
Sandy Lane Bay
St. George's Church
Payne's Bay
University of the West Indies
Grantley Adams Int. Airport
CHRIST CHURCH PARISH
N
E
W
S
ST. MICHAEL PARISH
Government House
Fresh Water Bay
Long Bay
Christ Church Church
1 Bridgetown
Government Headquarters
Oistins 2
The Careenage
Carlisle Bay
Needham Pt.
Hastings
Rockley
Worthing
St. Lawrence
Oistins Bay
South Point

Acknowledgements

Although most of the photographs for this book were taken in the early 1990s, this book is the product of more than fifteen years of visiting Barbados, and over that time I have received assistance and guidance from countless people on the island. As I have written before, Barbadians are an exceptionally open and gracious people, and that national personality makes the island a delight for a photojournalist to work in: more times than I can remember, Barbadians have given me access to their homes, property, records, hospitality, thoughts, and time in order to facilitate my photography, my research, or simply my understanding of Barbados. I am indebted to them all, and I hope they will find this book the better for their generosity, even if I cannot mention them all individually. I would be remiss, however, if I failed to acknowledge the following people and institutions, who have over the past years been unstinting in their support of my efforts to capture and interpret Barbados and her people: Kathleen Goddard; Jimmy and Jill Walker, Chris and Susan Trew, and all the people at Best of Barbados, Ltd.; Henry Fraser, Paul Foster, Paul Altman, and the many other people associated with the Barbados National Trust; Barbados Museum & Historical Society; Barbados Board of Tourism; and Jean and Suzanne Baulu. I also wish to thank Tim Sweeney, Charles Wattles, and Ella LaBrucherie for reviewing and commenting on the text. The photograph of the donkey cart in "King Sugar" is by Roy & Debbie Gerard.

Imágenes Press
Post Office Box 1080
Pine Valley, California 91962 USA
Tel: 619-473-8676/FAX: 619-473-8272

Design consultant: HOCHdesigns

Barbados, Sun, Sea, Superb!
ISBN 0-939302-30-6 (Deluxe Edition)
ISBN 0-939302-31-4 (Trade Edition)

Printed in China

2 4 5 3 1